I0163238

The Texas Adventures of Arnie Armadillo – Big Bend Country

Copyright © 2013 by Kathy Gause
Cover and internal design © Kathy Gause

All rights reserved. No part of this book may be reproduced in any form or by any electronic or mechanical means including information storage and retrieval systems – except in the case of brief quotations in articles or reviews – without the written permission in writing from its publisher, Kathy Gause.

All brand names and product names used in this book are trademarks, registered trademarks, or trade names of their respective holders. We are not associated with any product or vendor in this book.

About the Author

Kathy Gause is a retired nurse and freelance writer living in Irving, Texas. She comes from a long line of Texans, including Jesse Billingsley, who fought for Texas Independence alongside Sam Houston at the Battle of San Jacinto. She has been married to her best friend and love of her life, Paul, since 1983. Together, they have three grown children and four awesome grandchildren (Caden, Allison, Bricen, and Andrew). She dedicates all of her books to her grandchildren.

She welcomes any comments, suggestions, or criticisms. You can email her at k.gause@verizon.net. Also visit her website at www.ArnieArmadillo.com.

"A generation which ignores history has no past and no future."
- Robert Heinlein

Arnie was an armadillo from Missouri who had traveled to Texas in search of other armadillos. Shortly after arriving in Texas, he met Albert Armadillo and his family. Albert agreed to go with Arnie on a road trip around Texas to explore all the different regions of Texas. Arnie and Albert had already traveled through the Texas Piney Woods, the Texas Gulf Coast, the South Texas Plains, and the Texas Hill Country. They had just finished touring the Texas State Capitol in Austin and were now ready and excited to be traveling to the Big Bend Country.

Lake Amistad

Mexico

Texas

Arnie and Albert's first stop in the Big Bend region was the city of Del Rio. Del Rio is a border city located along the Rio Grande River. Directly across the Rio Grande River is the Mexican city called Cuidad Acuna.

Del Rio is home to Lake Amistad. Lake Amistad is unique in that three large rivers (the Rio Grande, the Pecos River, and the Devils River) combine to form it, making it the second largest lake in Texas. Also unique to Lake Amistad is the dam. The Lake Amistad Dam was built in 1969 and is owned by both the United States government and the Mexican government. The dam serves as an international bridge between Del Rio and Cuidad Acuna.

Not far from Del Rio is the Devils River State Natural Area. Arnie and Albert learned from a park ranger that this area is a favorite among hikers, campers, swimmers, and canoers. There are several springs where swimmers enjoy clear water. Arnie and Albert wanted to cool off in the hot Texas sun, so they went for a swim!

Arnie and Albert discovered that Seminole Canyon State Park was not too far away. They saw many raccoons, white-tailed deer, and squirrels. This area is very rocky and has deep canyons.

Native American Rock Paintings

This area is home to one of the oldest cave dwellings in the entire United States called the Fate Bell Shelter. Arnie and Albert were amazed at the Native American rock paintings inside this cave dwelling.

Arnie and Albert's next stop was the Big Bend National Park. The Big Bend National Park is the largest state park in Texas. For little more than a thousand miles, the Rio Grande River forms the international boundary between Mexico and the United States. This region of southwest Texas contains some species of plants, such as the Chisos Oak, that are found nowhere else in the United States.

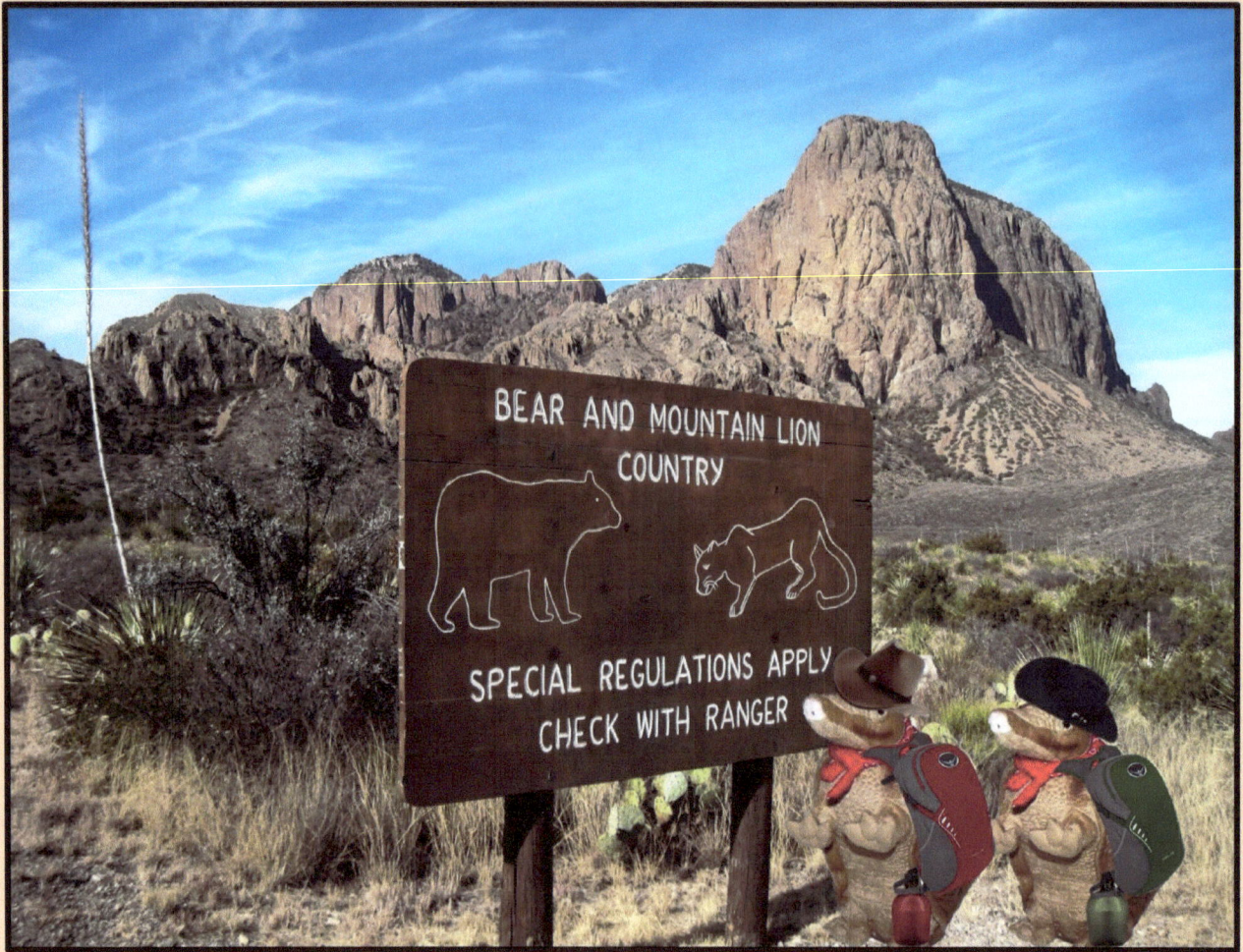

Arnie and Albert learned from one of the park rangers that they had to be prepared before traveling through the Big Bend National Park. "You must carry plenty of water because it would be easy to get lost while hiking and become dehydrated from not drinking enough water," said the park ranger. "In the desert areas of the Big Bend, it gets hot during the day and very cool at night," explained the ranger. So Arnie and Albert packed their backpacks, filled their water bottles, and set out for their long hike of the Big Bend.

As they hiked along, they were amazed at the beauty of the Big Bend. There were many different plants, such as the Century plant which only blooms once in its life time, and they can live up to 100 years. Then it spreads its seeds and dies.

There were also cacti called "Cholla." This cactus has sharp spines or barbs that can catch on your clothing as you walk by it. The blooms on the cholla are pink, yellow, purple, or red.

While they were stopped for a water break, Arnie and Albert met a mother bear and her three babies which are called cubs. "Hello! My name is Bonnie and these are my cubs – Brindle, Bubba, and Buddy." "Hello!" replied Arnie and Albert. "Where are you going?" asked Arnie. "We are looking for food. We love to eat the pine nuts, madrone berries, and acorns which are plentiful here in the Big Bend," said Bonnie. "However, I really love to eat prickly pear fruit and yucca," she laughed. The bear cubs were quite playful and rowdy! After visiting with Bonnie and her cubs for a short time, Arnie and Albert said their goodbyes and continued on their hike.

Arnie and Albert saw so many different insects, reptiles, and spiders. Of course, since armadillos love to eat insects, they had to taste a few! They ate a few "Lubber Grasshoppers" and even a few Lady Bugs! One of the most interesting bugs they saw was the "Velvet Mite." This tiny insect lives underground except for a few hours each year. It will come out of the ground after a heavy rain. Arnie was able to get some great pictures of some of these insects.

When Arnie and Albert made it to the Santa Elena Canyon, they decided to go for a canoe ride down the Rio Grande River. So far, Arnie and Albert were really enjoying their exploration of the Big Bend National Park.

After leaving the Chisos Basin, Arnie and Albert came upon Fort Leaton State Historical Park. They learned from a park ranger that this fort was originally built in 1848 and served as a trading post. The ranger told them "carretas" (or large ox carts) were used to transport goods and freight along the Chihuahua Trail to San Antonio. The wheels of this carreta were taller than Arnie and Albert!

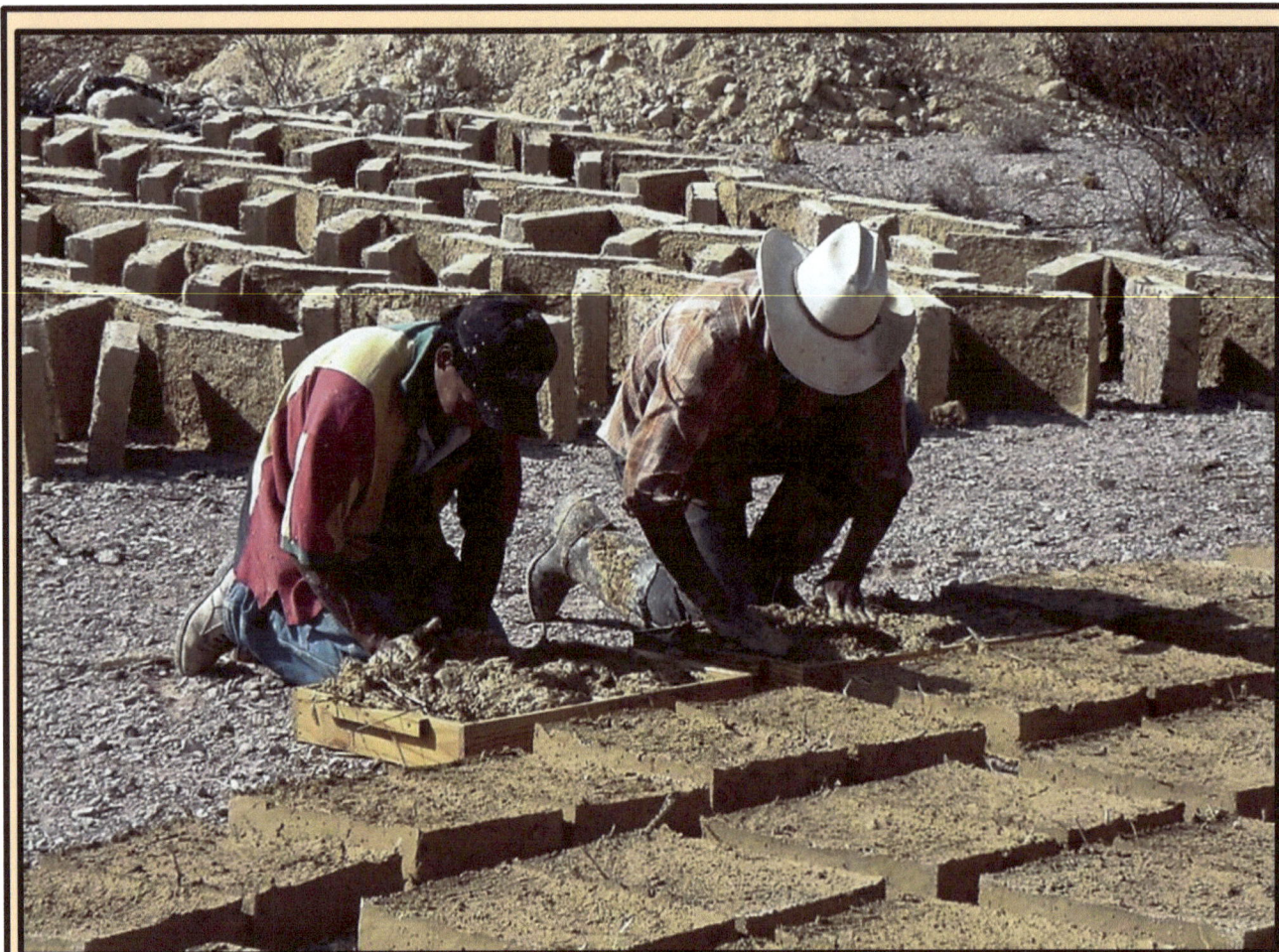

"This fort was built from adobe," said the park ranger. He explained to them how adobe was made. "Adobe is a mixture of straw, water, and clay that is precast into wooden forms," said the ranger. "After setting and hardening for a time, the adobe is removed from the forms and allowed to dry thoroughly in the hot desert sun. The 'bricks' are then plastered together using mud mortar." He added, "These adobe walls hold the coolness in the summer and the warmth in the winter."

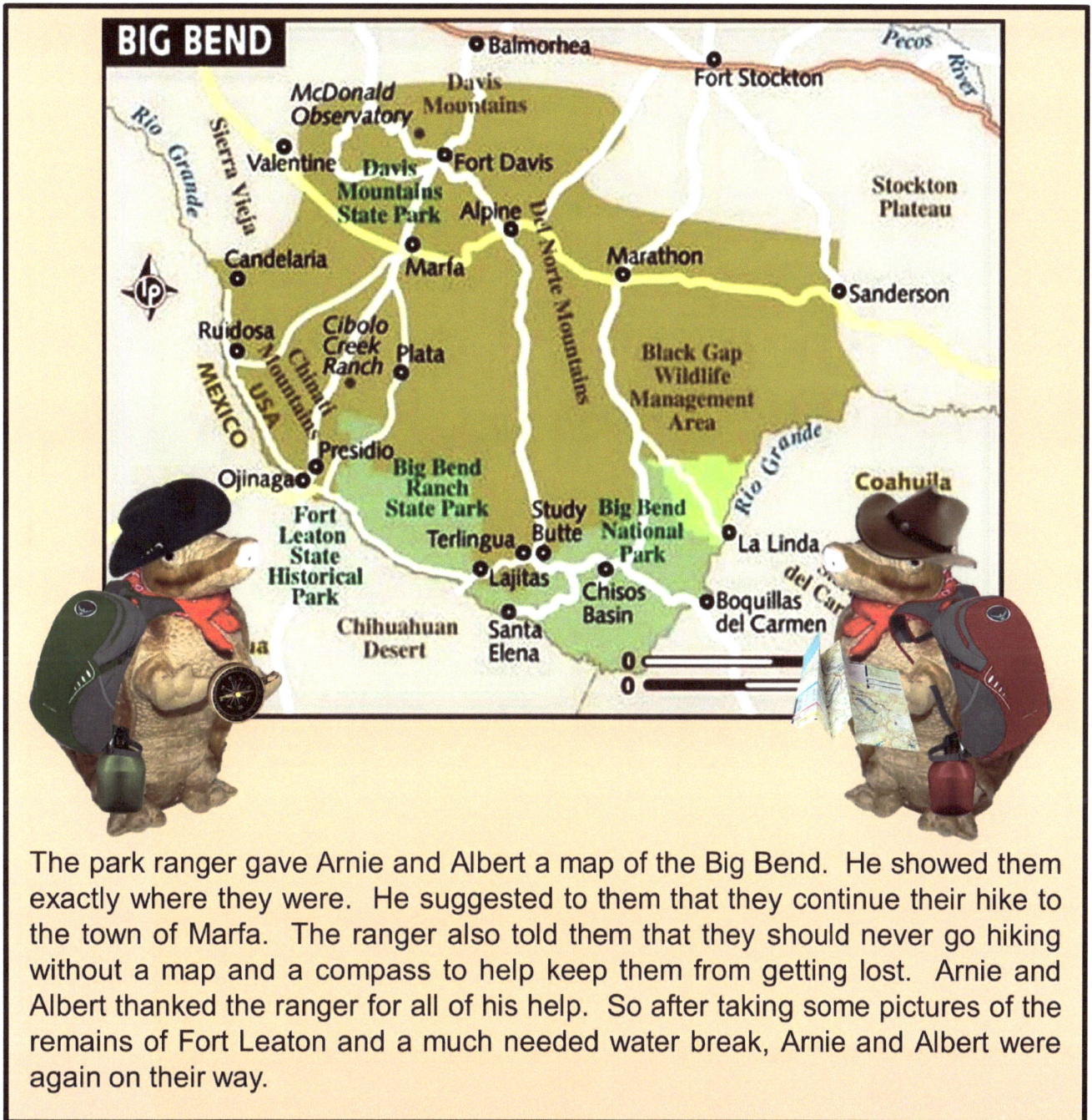

The park ranger gave Arnie and Albert a map of the Big Bend. He showed them exactly where they were. He suggested to them that they continue their hike to the town of Marfa. The ranger also told them that they should never go hiking without a map and a compass to help keep them from getting lost. Arnie and Albert thanked the ranger for all of his help. So after taking some pictures of the remains of Fort Leaton and a much needed water break, Arnie and Albert were again on their way.

As they hiked along, Arnie and Albert met a coyote. "Howdy! My name is Caden," the coyote said. "Coyotes live in underground dens and eat gophers, squirrels, mice, rabbits, frogs, snakes, and occasionally nuts and berries. We like to bark, yip, growl, yap, and howl to communicate with each other," yapped Caden. Caden showed Arnie and Albert how he can leap into the air up to fourteen feet. Arnie and Albert were most impressed since they could only jump up three to four feet! Arnie and Albert enjoyed talking to Caden, but they had to say goodbye so they could be on their way again. Caden told them, "Nice to meet you. Hope to see you again sometime!"

A little ways down the hiking trail, Arnie and Albert were startled by a growling mountain lion. Arnie and Albert were afraid because the park ranger had told them to be careful of mountain lions. But the mountain lion spoke saying, "My name is Manny. If I hadn't just eaten lunch, I would be interested in eating you, but my stomach is full," he growled. Arnie and Albert breathed a big sigh of relief! Manny told them he lives alone, and he prefers to eat deer and javelina. Arnie and Albert quickly said their goodbyes and went on their way! They were afraid that Manny would change his mind about being hungry!

Arnie and Albert hadn't hiked too far when they were startled again by a low meowing in the brush. Out popped a different type of cat called a bobcat. "Howdy! My name is Bricen," said the bobcat. Arnie and Albert cautiously asked Bricen if he was hungry! "I don't generally eat armadillos. I mostly eats rats, squirrels, birds, rabbits, and lizards," answered Bricen. Arnie and Albert relaxed a bit and told Bricen about the mountain lion they had just seen. "Wow! Y'all better be careful," Bricen said as he walked away. Arnie and Albert shouted, "Nice to meet you!" and went on their way.

After getting back in their truck, they came to the town of Marfa. Marfa is best known for its strange and mysterious dancing lights. They decided to visit the town's visitors' center. They talked with a lady behind the counter about the lights. She told them, "No one has been able to figure out what causes these lights. They are sometimes red, sometimes blue, and sometimes white." She also told them that these lights appear at random throughout the night, no matter what the weather is like.

After seeing these strange and unexplainable lights for themselves, Arnie and Albert headed out of town towards the Davis Mountains State Park. The park ranger had told Arnie and Albert to be sure to visit the McDonald Observatory where they could view the stars from huge, powerful telescopes. Arnie and Albert were speechless when they looked through these powerful telescopes and saw the stars up close.

Arnie and Albert's next stop was the Fort Davis National Historic Site. This fort is one of the best surviving examples of an Indian Wars' frontier military post in the Southwestern United States. Fort Davis protected the mail coaches, travelers, and freight wagons from the Indian War parties. Today, it stands as a living history fort where volunteers dress in period clothing and re-enact what life was like during the 1880's. Arnie and Albert were able to go for a ride in a covered wagon!

From Fort Davis, Arnie and Albert began their long trek to El Paso. This city sits on the border of West Texas, New Mexico, and the country of Mexico. El Paso was known as the Wild West. The city grew quickly during the Old West days of gunslingers. It was a popular place for infamous characters such as Billy the Kid, Pancho Villa, and Wyatt Earp, as well as the Texas Rangers. Today, it is the largest American city on the Mexican border and is full of culture and diversity. Nowhere else in Texas is quite like it!

El Paso is home to the Hueco Tanks State Park and Historic Site. Hueco is Spanish for "hollows" and was so named because of the hollows that formed in the rocks. For the protection of the natural and cultural resources at this park, Arnie and Albert had to get special permission from the park rangers to explore it.

Centuries ago, Native Americans painted their stories on the rocks. These paintings are called pictographs. The park ranger said, "You should never touch pictographs because the oil from your hands will damage them. It is wrong to destroy these ancient paintings by adding graffiti of your own," This park area is still used by Native Americans for their traditional cultural activities and performances. Arnie and Albert were fortunate enough to be able to watch some of the Native American performances. They found a group of large boulders to sit on. Arnie took some great photos!

Barrel Cactus

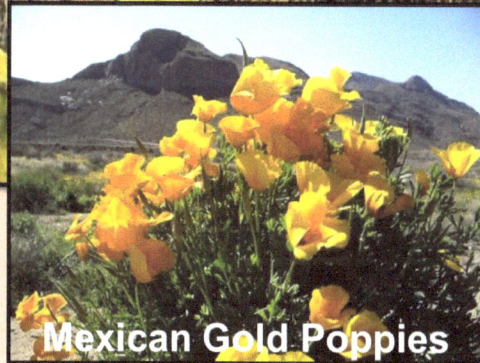

Mexican Gold Poppies

The Franklin Mountains State Park is also not far from El Paso. The Franklin Mountains is the largest mountain range in Texas. Arnie and Albert learned that the Mexican Gold Poppies bloom all over the hillsides in early spring. The park ranger said, "The large southwestern barrel cactus found throughout the park can grow up to six feet tall!"

Arnie and Albert learned that the only place in Texas where you'll find a public tramway is in the Franklin Mountains. They wanted to go for a ride on the Wylie Aerial Tramway. So they decided to just that! Arnie was a little nervous because it's so high up, but he did just fine. Arnie and Albert learned that the tramway car is called a gondola. The view from so high up was spectacular! They could see for miles and miles!

Arnie and Albert continued on their way to Pine Springs. Pine Springs is a small town which, in its' early days, was the location of a station on the famous stagecoach run, Butterfield Overland Mail Route, which ran from St. Louis, Missouri to San Francisco, California. For several months, these Butterfield stagecoaches would stop here for water, food, rest, fresh mule teams, and protection. Each coach traveled day and night and carried nine passengers, essential baggage, and 12,000 letters. The only things that remain of the station are parts of the stone walls.

El Capitan

Pine Springs is also home to the Guadalupe Mountains State Park. The top of Guadalupe Peak is the highest point in Texas. The most prominent summit is called "El Capitan." The park ranger said, "There is a big difference between the different areas of the 'Guads,' as they are called by the local people." Arnie and Albert learned there are woodland canyons and rugged wilderness. The temperature can change very quickly from hot to cold. These mountains are a popular place for hikers, campers, stargazers, and horseback riders.

One of the favorite areas that Arnie and Albert found in the Guadalupe Mountains was McKittrick Canyon. The fall colors in this area are absolutely beautiful! Arnie was able to get some really great pictures!

It was in McKittrick Canyon where Arnie and Albert came across a fox-like creature. "Hello, my name is Katy, and I am a Kit fox," she said. "Kit foxes live in dens. In fact, we usually have more than one den at a time." Arnie asked, "Do you eat armadillos?" Katy replied, "No, I like to eat rabbits, mice, birds, and an occasional insect. I am not normally out during the day. I am nocturnal," she explained. "Nocturnal means being active at night and asleep during the day," Arnie explained to Albert. Katy yawned and politely said, "I must go home and sleep so I will be able to hunt tonight." They said their goodbyes and went their separate ways.

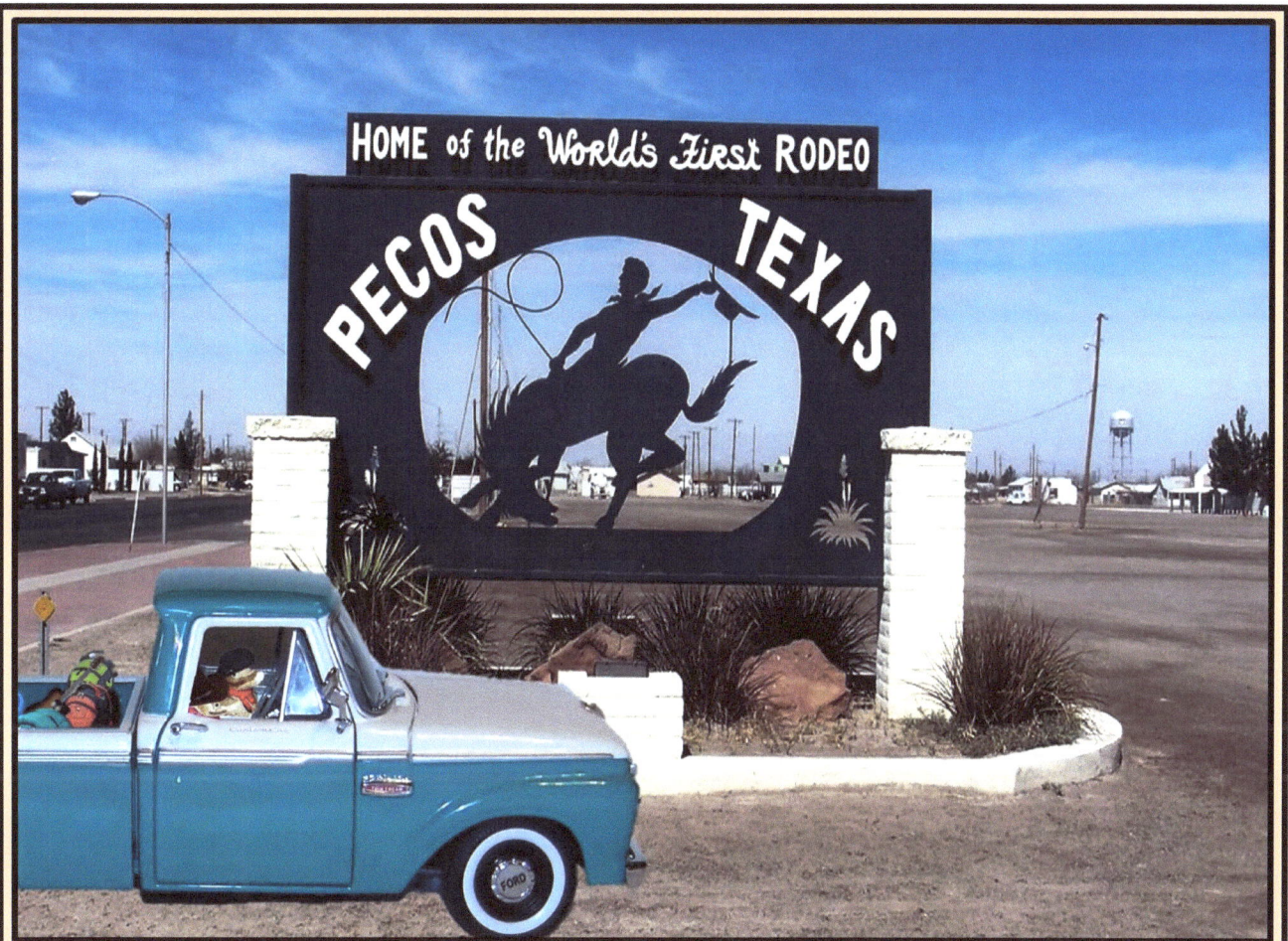

After finishing their hike, Arnie and Albert climbed back into their truck and headed down the road. Their next stop was the town of Pecos. Pecos claims to be the "Home of the World's First Rodeo." On July 4, 1883, cowboys from a few cattle outfits competed against each other to see who was the fastest steer roper. Prizes for the winners were blue ribbons cut from a new dress of a four year old girl watching this "rodeo." Arnie and Albert had seen several rodeos during their travels through the Texas regions. They loved rodeos and thought they were lots of fun.

Pecos is also famous for its cantaloupes. The Pecos cantaloupe has a distinctive flavor. Arnie and Albert found a little refreshment stand in downtown Pecos and decided to try the "Cantaloupe Cooler." "Ummm," Arnie exclaimed! "This is very refreshing!"

Just a little ways down the street from where they were was the "West of the Pecos" Museum. This museum resides in the Orient Hotel which was built in 1896 and used as a saloon first and then as a hotel in 1904. It claimed to be the "Finest from Ft. Worth to El Paso." This museum consists of three floors that contain over fifty rooms of Native American artifacts, historical items, railroad artifacts, and items related to cowboys, rodeos, and "Pecos Bill." Arnie and Albert saw some very fascinating things here!

As they left Pecos, they drove across the Pecos River. This river extends from the western slope of the Sante Fe mountain range in New Mexico winding down to the Rio Grande River in the Amistad Reservoir not far from Del Rio, Texas. This river is popular with canoeists, kayakers, hikers, campers, and rafters. Arnie and Albert decided this would be a great spot to camp for the night. Arnie and Albert were going to miss this part of Texas, but there was still so much more for them to see!

After Arnie and Albert got the tent together, they gathered firewood to make a fire. They had learned how to make a fire and how to be safe around a campfire from one of the park rangers earlier in their journey. He had also taught them how to roast marshmallows. Arnie and Albert loved to roast marshmallows! After eating, they planned to sing some campfire songs and stargaze, but storm clouds were gathering. It was a good thing they had the tent to take shelter in and plenty of blankets! Armadillos don't like cold weather!

From Pecos, Arnie and Albert's journey would next take them to the town of Monahans, the home of Monahans Sandhills State Park. The active sand dunes in this park grow and change shape in response to the changing winds. "This is a popular place for visitors to sand sled," said the park ranger. "You can rent some disks to sled down the sand dunes," the ranger said. Arnie and Albert jumped at the chance to do something that sounded and looked like so much fun! The ranger was right – they had a lot of fun!

From the Monahans Sandhills State Park, they made it to the city of Odessa. Odessa is part of what is known as the "Permian Basin." The Permian Basin is an oil field that covers an area about 250 miles wide and 300 miles long located in West Texas and southwestern New Mexico. The first commercial oil well started pumping in Odessa in 1921.

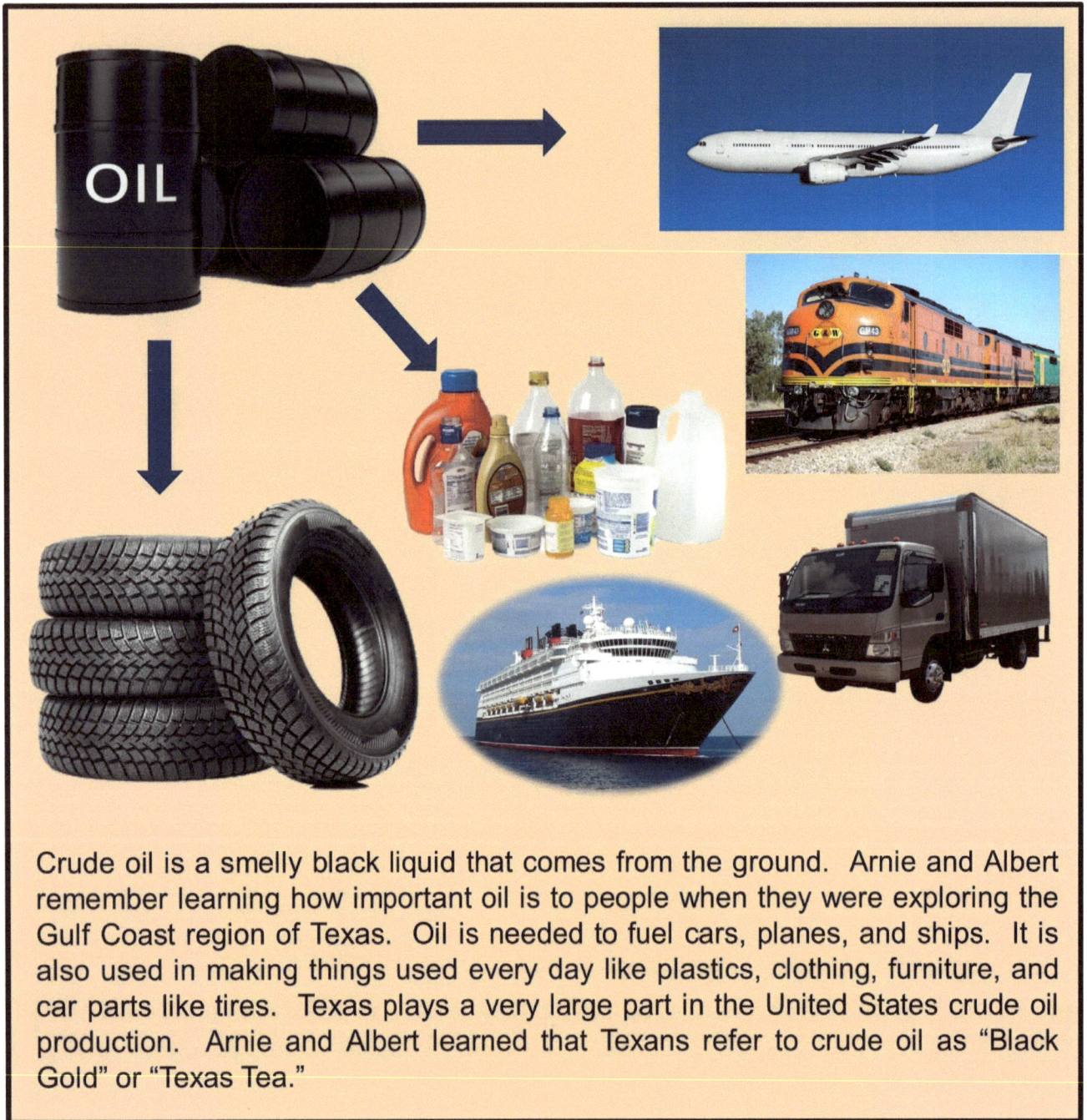

Crude oil is a smelly black liquid that comes from the ground. Arnie and Albert remember learning how important oil is to people when they were exploring the Gulf Coast region of Texas. Oil is needed to fuel cars, planes, and ships. It is also used in making things used every day like plastics, clothing, furniture, and car parts like tires. Texas plays a very large part in the United States crude oil production. Arnie and Albert learned that Texans refer to crude oil as "Black Gold" or "Texas Tea."

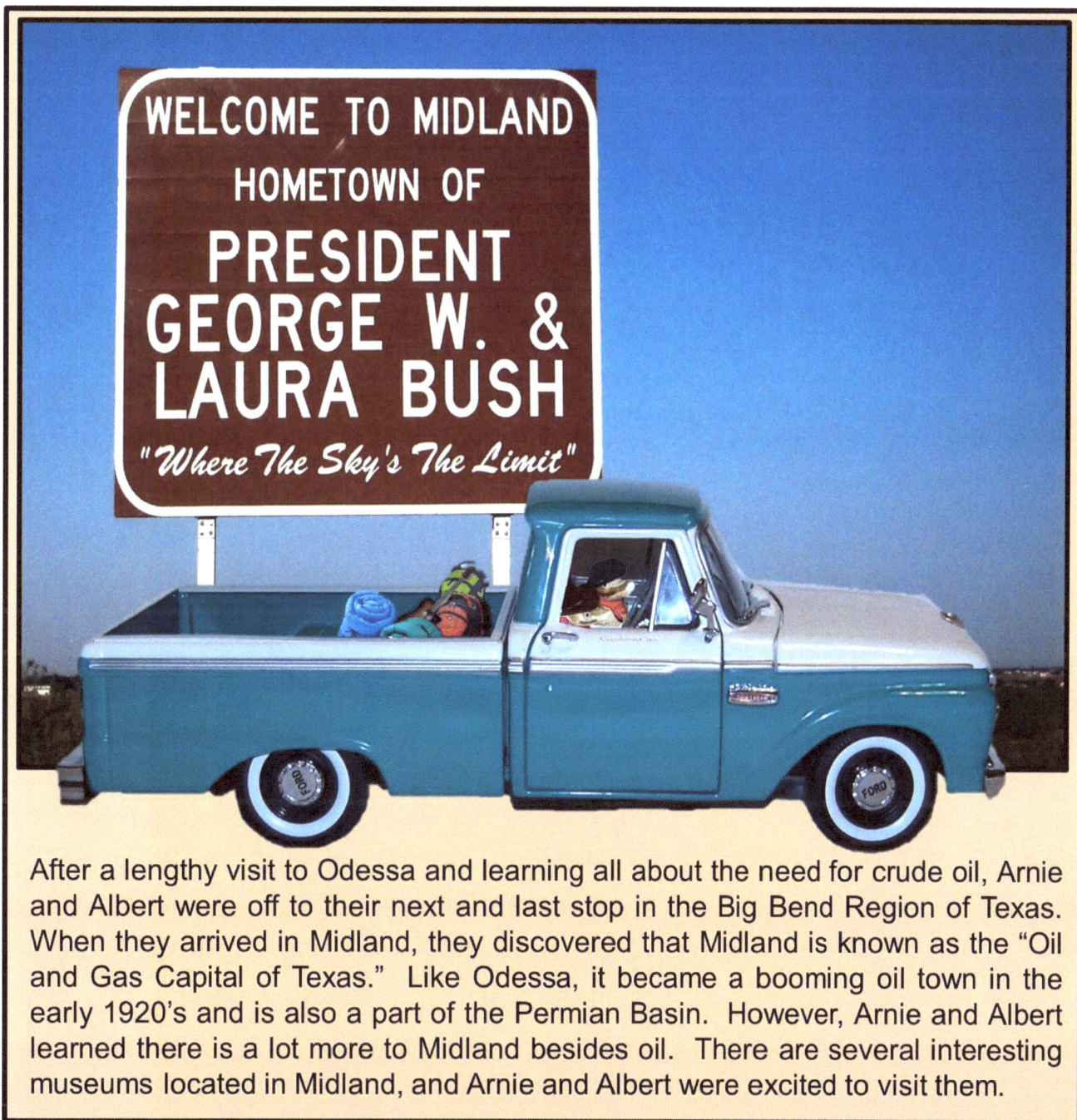

After a lengthy visit to Odessa and learning all about the need for crude oil, Arnie and Albert were off to their next and last stop in the Big Bend Region of Texas. When they arrived in Midland, they discovered that Midland is known as the "Oil and Gas Capital of Texas." Like Odessa, it became a booming oil town in the early 1920's and is also a part of the Permian Basin. However, Arnie and Albert learned there is a lot more to Midland besides oil. There are several interesting museums located in Midland, and Arnie and Albert were excited to visit them.

The first museum they visited was the childhood home of the 43rd President of the United States, George W. Bush. This home has been restored to portray the way the house looked when the Bush family was living here in the 1950's. As Arnie and Albert were touring the house, they came across this strange looking box with a green glass screen on it. Arnie asked the tour guide what it was and she told them, "Why, that's a very old television." Albert told Arnie, "It has such a small screen!" Arnie and Albert learned a lot about what life was like during the 1950's.

George H. W. and Barbara Bush
41st President of the United States

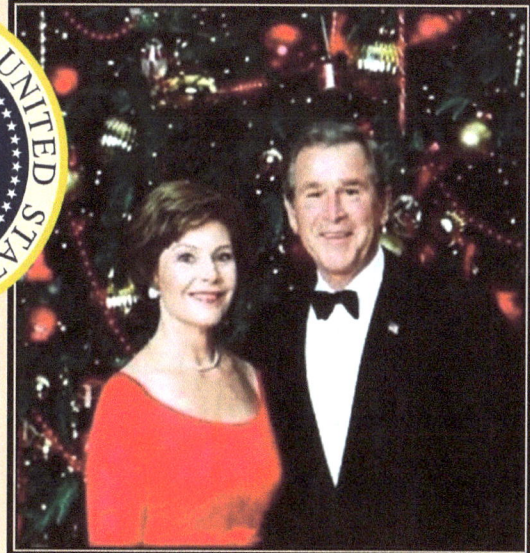

George W. and Laura Bush
43rd President of the United States
Governor of Texas from 1995 to 2000

The White House in Washington D. C.
(Home of the Current President of the United States)

This house celebrates the lives of two U. S. Presidents. They were George W. Bush, the 43rd President and his father, George H. W. Bush, the 41st President. Their wives are Laura and Barbara Bush. Arnie and Albert also learned that George W. Bush was the Governor of Texas from January 1995 to December 2000, resigning as governor in the middle of his second term to become President of the United States.

Arnie and Albert's next stop was the CAF Airpower Museum. This museum tells the story of World War II military aviation (airplanes and helicopters). There is also a Vietnam War Memorial which contains fighter jets and helicopters flown during this war. Arnie got to sit in the cockpit of one of the World War II airplanes.

Antique gas pump

After their adventures in the CAF Airpower Museum, Arnie and Albert set off for the Permian Basin Petroleum Museum. This museum tells the story of petroleum (crude oil). There were many interesting exhibits here, as well as old photos from long ago of the oil industry. Arnie was looking at one photo showing an antique car and something tall next to it. He asked one of the museum workers what it was. The museum worker laughed and told him, "Why that's what gas pumps used to look like!"

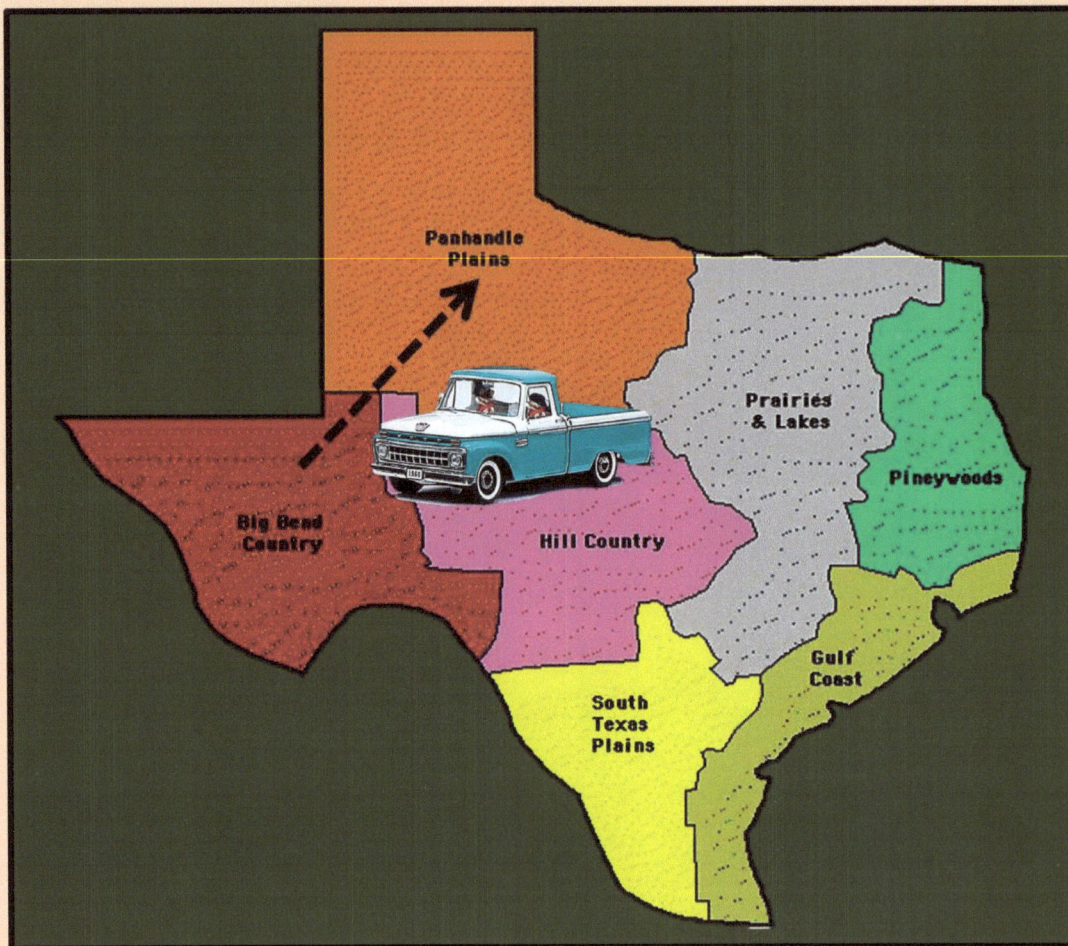

Arnie and Albert's adventures in the Big Bend Country were over. They had made many new friends and had such wonderful experiences to share with Albert's family when they got back home. Arnie had taken a lot of pictures to add to his scrapbook. Arnie and Albert were sorry to leave the Big Bend Country, but they were very excited to begin their next adventures in the Texas Panhandle Plains. Be sure to join them as they journey through the canyon lands and the Old West heritage of the Panhandle Plains.

The Adventures of Arnie Armadillo

If you enjoyed this book, be sure to read Arnie's other books which tell the stories of his adventures all over the State of Texas!

Texas Adventure Series:
- The Adventures of Arnie Armadillo in the State of Texas
- The Texas Adventures of Arnie Armadillo – Texas Piney Woods
- The Texas Adventures of Arnie Armadillo – Texas Gulf Coast
- The Texas Adventures of Arnie Armadillo – South Texas Plains
- The Texas Adventures of Arnie Armadillo – Texas Hill Country
- The Texas Adventures of Arnie Armadillo – Big Bend Country
- The Texas Adventures of Arnie Armadillo – Texas Panhandle Plains
- The Texas Adventures of Arnie Armadillo – Texas Prairies and Lakes
- The Texas Adventures of Arnie Armadillo in the Texas State Capitol

Texas Heroes Series:
- Samuel "Sam" Houston
- Jose Antonio Navarro
- Stephen F. Austin
- James "Jim" Bowie
- Davy Crockett
- Lorenzo de Zavala
- Thomas Jefferson Rusk
- Juan Seguin
- Mirabeau B. Lamar
- Anson Jones
- James Fannin
- William B. Travis

www.ingramcontent.com/pod-product-compliance
Lightning Source LLC
Chambersburg PA
CBHW042058040426
42448CB00002B/59